Situational Survival Gear:

Lessons to Stay Safe in Dangerous Situations

Table of Contents

Introduction

How aware are you of your surrounding environment?

This might surprise you, but situational awareness can end up saving your life during an adverse situation. It is the ability to identify, comprehend, and process every vital sign around you in order to survive and come out of a dangerous situation.

Every survivor out there should get acquainted with situational awareness and harness the power of their instincts with time. The concept might be new to you, but it is taken seriously by most of the military units around the world. Special force officers are trained to develop their situational awareness skills, particularly during an emergency.

Situation awareness is hard to maintain and is quite easy to lose, which makes it so dynamic in nature. Don't worry! We are here to help you. We know without gaining productive knowledge about your surroundings, you can't truly survive a disaster. In this guide, we will help you learn how you can maintain situational awareness even in the worst-case scenario.

From different combat rules to psychological analysis, we have covered it all. Clear your mind and buckle up your belt for you are about to bring a much-needed change in your life!

Chapter 1 – The Importance Of Situational Awareness

Do you ever wonder how some trained individuals are able to come out of an extreme situation without much trouble? What kind of attribute makes them so unique?

Well, it is not only their will or sense of determination that makes them a true survivor, but also the way they perceive their surrounding environment and stay focused all the time. If you want to be a true survivor, then you should definitely learn how to develop your situational awareness skills as well.

In a nutshell, Situational Awareness (or commonly known as SA) is the art of knowing what's happening around you and taking subsequent actions in the most feasible manner. It is definitely an art in itself, as it requires some time to develop and is pretty hard to nurture.

SA is basically the way an individual perceives their surrounding elements and how they are able to comprehend its meaning. All of this is done while projecting a change in order to predict an upcoming event. Yes, it is not a piece of cake, as it leads to critical decision making, especially in an emergency situation.

From fighting to surviving a disaster, your situational awareness can be a driving force in plenty of ways. There are different levels of situational awareness that are classified with respect to the way one "feels" every aspect related to a situation. The following projection of the Endsley model will let you know how vast the concept of situational awareness can be.

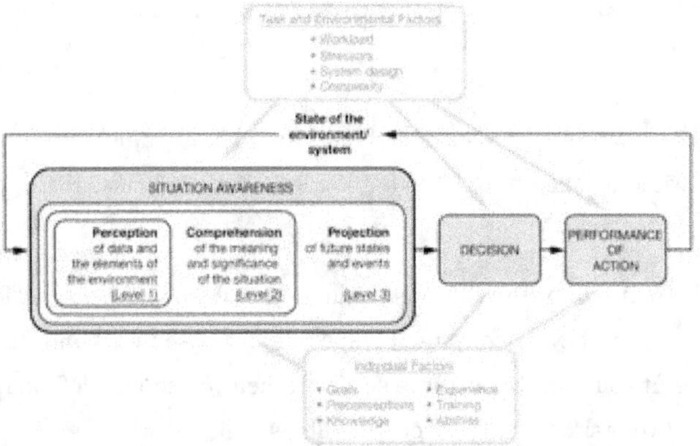

As stated, perception, comprehension, and projection are the three main levels of SA. Initially, one needs to perceive every kind of data related to their environment which leads to extracting knowledge about the significance of that respective situation. Subsequently, it leads to projecting the future events and results in decision-making.

Additionally, different factors like individual goals and environmental aspects can have a radical impact on SA. If you are not aware of your surroundings, then you might end up in a disastrous situation. All of this makes SA a vital sense that every individual should posses.

After getting to know the basics of situational awareness, you can already relate to its wide range of applications. From your everyday activities to those well-prepared combats, it can help you in numerous ways. Here's why SA it considered so important for every individual.

- There is a reason why SA plays a crucial role in military training. It can increase the combat skills of any individual to a whole new level. If you get attacked by someone unexpectedly, then you can definitely use your SA skills and win that fight.

- This might surprise you, but every traveler should focus on their survival skills and situational awareness as well. With so much happening around us, you might run into an unwanted situation anytime. If you are an avid traveler, then you should definitely focus on reading your environment to keep yourself safe.

- You might face an unexpected event at any time of the day. It doesn't matter if you are lost in the woods or are in the middle of a natural disaster, without your situational awareness, you won't be able to make it home.

- Situational awareness not only helps one to cope up with an ongoing event, but it can also prepare you for a post-event phase. After knowing everything, you can certainly come out of a disastrous situation both physically and psychologically.

- Even if you are entering an unexplored place or territory, your SA skills can drastically make things in your favor. You can learn about certain geography or its surrounding elements promptly.

- It is better to be safe than sorry. If you are training to be a survivor, then you should definitely sharpen your SA skills to come out of a disaster alive and help your loved ones at the same time.

- Most importantly, situational awareness can not only help you to come out of a drastic situation, but it can also let you avoid it altogether as well. We keep running into unexpected scenarios almost every single day. If you have an elevated sense of awareness, then you can definitely skip or avoid a dangerous situation.

From avoiding a potential threat to simply coming out of an adverse situation as a survivor, there are endless reasons to develop your SA skills. Now when you know about all these amazing benefits of having situational awareness, you are ready to commence your training. Read on and learn how to improve your situational awareness in due time.

Chapter 2 – The Rule Of Three

Situational Awareness is closely related to other significant aspects of survival skills. In order to truly make the most out of your senses, it is important to get familiar with some important facts. The rule of three is a popular theory that every survivor should know of.

Always remember, you can stay alive for 3 minutes without having oxygen in your brain – you can survive for 3 hours without being protected from the harshness of the environment – you can go on for 3 days without water, and 3 weeks without food. When you are in the middle of a disaster, you should definitely keep a track of time while utilizing the available resources.

The U.S. Military has a "Survival and Stop" thumb rule that you should also practice during an emergency situation.

• S: Scale the situation

• U: Utilize your senses

• R: Recall where you are present

• V: Vanish panic and fear

• I: Improve your situation

• V: Value-up your living

• A: Act like a native

• L: Learn basic skills

All of this can't be done without following the basic STOP methodology. It stands for:

• S: Sit

- T: Think

- O: Observe

- P: Plan

Memorize this sequence as it can save your life when you are fighting for your chance of survival. No matter how bad the situation is, if you are aware of your surroundings, then you can definitely come up with a productive plan. Just keep thinking of the "Survival" and "Stop" principle.

SIT

Whenever it seems that you are lost or are in the middle of an unwanted situation, you need to stop what you are doing. Just sit down for a while and try to relax. You can't make a rational decision just like that, as it might backfire you in the long haul.

Your health should be your first priority. Have a look at your body and try to move different parts to check if you have any internal injuries or not. If you are bleeding, then you need to make it stop. Subsequently, have a look around and try to connect with others. This is the time when you need to regulate your breathing and heartbeat, so that you can prepare yourself for the next step.

THINK

After taking a control over your senses, it is time to think of every possible situation. Try to learn how you got into that situation and what can be your best plan of action. This is the time when you need to prioritize things, as you won't be having an abundance of resources.

OBSERVE

After thinking of different plans, try to observe your environment. If you are in the woods or a natural environment, then chances are that you can use the nearby natural resources to survive. Even if you are in a combat zone, you need to observe the situation and need to lay focus on every minute detail. This would help you in order to come up with a plan of action.

PLAN

Lastly, after thinking everything straight and observing the situation wisely, think of a bulletproof plan. You need to contemplate a little, but would have to think fast while coming up with a plan. Meanwhile, also come up with a Plan B, in case you face an unexpected situation. This will help you prepare for the worst-case scenario.

<u>Modern Urban Combat Tactics</u>

We all live in an urban jungle. Chances are that you might face an unexpected situation in an urban area rather than getting lost in the woods. Though, you can always apply the STOP technique in an urban combat, but there are a few other tactics that you should always keep in mind.

Here are some thoughtful tricks (Rule of 3) related to Modern Urban Combat Tactics, or commonly known as MUCT.

3 things to defend yourself

Before you start any combat, make sure that you have a defense mechanism. Think of 3 things that can help you to defend yourself. It can be anything from a weapon to a common household tool. Ideally, you should try to carry a knife or a metal pen with you in order to defend yourself.

3 strikes for each block

Always follow this rule of thumb when you are in a combat. This is something which distinguishes professionals from novices. After when you block an attack, follow it up with three consecutive strikes. This would let your opponent know that you are not aiming to give up and can strike back with more force after getting attacked.

3 different targets

When you are striking or attacking your component, try to avoid hitting the same target consecutively. Your target could be in the same general area, but it should be different than the previous one. Don't just fixate yourself to a certain area while attacking to get optimum results.

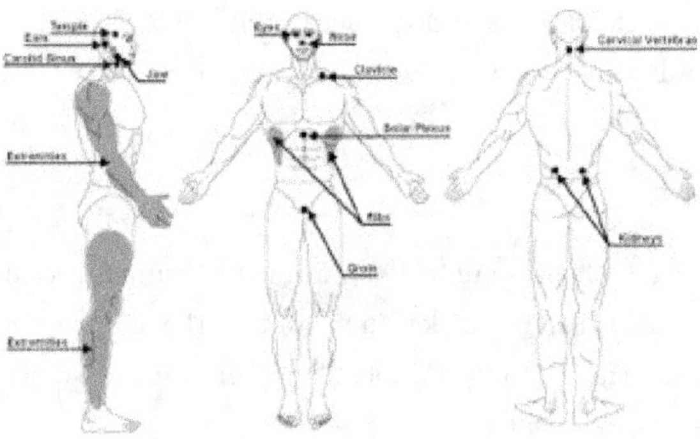

3 body zones

Our body is made up of three different zones, which you should keep in while attacking someone. The first zone is from the head to the collarbones, middle zone is from the shoulders to the waist, and lower zone is groin and below.

3 weapons

Even while attacking, you should get yourself acquainted with at least 3 different types of weapons. It could be anything from a stick to a knife that you can keep handy. Try to be a little diverse and train yourself with at least three weapons to master the art of urban combat.

The Rule of Three would certainly come handy to you on numerous occasions. Not only would it be of a great help to tackle urban combat, but it can also help you while overcoming a worst-case scenario. Needless to say, it is the foundation of Situational Awareness and forms the first steps towards your SA training.

After following all the above-mentioned suggestions, step it up and learn how you can access your environment in the next chapter.

Chapter 3 – Decoding Your Environment

Accessing your surrounding environment is probably the first thing that can help you analyze a situation. There are different steps associated with it, which might differ from one situation to another. Nevertheless, it doesn't matter if you are caught in an urban fire or if you are trying to find your way home, these suggestions would certainly help you a lot in order to decode your surroundings.

Look for any potential threat

Before you try to come up with a plan, always look for any potential threat that might be present in your surrounding environment. This is the first step to increasing your SA ability. This can't be done without focusing on every minute detail around you, which might differ from one environment to another.

Always make an effort and keep looking for any possible risk. For instance, if you are in the woods, then you need to be aware of wild animals and poisonous insects. If you are in the snow, then you need to be aware of thin ice. Similarly, if you are in an urban location, you need to be aware of a concrete structure, a hollow floor, or a false ceiling.

Think of an ideal situation around you

This particularly helps if you are in chaos or a disastrous situation. What should be the baseline or a normal situation around you? Try to think of how the environment should ideally behave in order to understand the differences. Keep the ideal situation as a reference and then compare it with an unusual change.

For instance, if you are in the woods, then the baseline would be the sound of the animals and birds or the smell of the forest. Any change in it can help you identify a potential threat. Similarly, the baseline of any urban area would be the sound of the vehicles and crowded places. Understand the ideal situation carefully in order to recognize the differences.

Estimate dangerous elements around you

After identifying all the surrounding threats and comparing them with the ideal situation, you would be able to gauge the impact any unwanted element can cause around you. It is of utmost importance that you compare it with the baseline and the surrounding elements to identify every kind of dangerous entity around you.

If you are surrounded by others, then look for those people who are behaving in a suspicious way and compare them with their ideal behavior. Identify the individuals having a weapon and try to measure the kind of impact they can cause in the surrounding environment.

Sometimes, people can conceal a weapon or can just hide it. Try to look beyond the obvious and search for the imprint of these weapons on their clothes. Learn to look nearby the waistband, where most of the people carry their concealed weapons. Additionally, search for bags or any explosive object that should not be left in a public place. Try to measure its impact in order to devise a plan of action.

Act as per the environment

This is where you would be asked to use your imagination. After analyzing the impact of any dangerous entity, you need to think of different ways to optimize it. Think of various alternatives and how the other individual or entity would react after your action.

This will help you to come up with different scenarios and you would learn to address them by devising their impact one step at a time. For instance, if you see someone drawing a weapon, try to think of a counter attack or a defense strategy.

If you see a group of people heading towards you, then you need to think what could be their way of attempting things and how you can outdo them. If the current environment is getting pretty hostile, then think of a way to leave it as fast as you can.

Nevertheless, you need to do all of this in a second. Situation awareness is all about making the right call in less time. You need to observe, think, and plan in a matter of a few seconds and make it work to truly make the most out of your environment.

We are sure that these suggestions would certainly help you to access your surroundings. After decoding your environment, learn how to harness your focus and attention in the next chapter.

Chapter 4 – Stay Focused

Staying focused and being attentive is the key to harnessing your situational awareness. Though, after accessing your environment, you can surely gain a lot of productive knowledge that can help you during your decision-making, but it won't be enough. You can't act quickly or decode your surroundings without staying focused.

In order to come up with a foolproof plan, you need to focus on every minute detail. Most of the people have the attention span of just 12 seconds. That can't really help you in an emergency situation. Take the help of the following suggestions and learn how to stay focused.

Don't take anything for granted

Since most of us live a fairly simple world, we don't consider anything abnormal as a threat. Whenever you recognize any abnormal behavior in your environment, you should not take it for granted. Instead, be more focused and don't make any presumptions. Approach the situation wisely and consider its threats in the back of your mind.

Avoid Distractions

Whenever you are too focused on anything, you seem to overlook the rest of the entities present in the environment. This is known as a "focus lock". Though you might attain in-depth knowledge regarding a certain entity, but might overlook the bigger picture while doing so.

A classic example of this is a situation when you are too focused on your phone while driving or crossing the street. Too many times, while hiking, we get so distracted by the view or the sound of the forest that we walk into a trap.

Whenever you think you are getting too focused on something, try to draw away your attention. Try to look at the overall environment as it might possess some hidden threats.

It's all about the right timing!

Whenever you are accessing your environment, pay extra attention to the time. Focusing on the passage of time is quite vital in situational awareness. It can drastically help you to identify the behavior of others and recognize any unusual event. Also, during an extreme situation, it can help you keep the track of your eating or sleeping habits.

Even in everyday situations, you should always keep a track of time. For instance, if you are with your kids and have let them go somewhere, then you can act instantly if any adverse situation arises. Additionally, in a combat, if you are trying to attack someone, you should wait for the time when they are most vulnerable. It can help you save your life and optimize your efforts.

Complacency kills

"Complacency kills" is a widely known saying in the army. If you get too comfortable with a situation, then you won't be active enough to identify an upcoming threat. Even professionals make this mistake and try to get comfortable with a certain situation. You should always remember that complacency can never let you stay at the top of your game.

Every time you get comfortable with a certain situation, you stop looking beyond the obvious. This is exactly when you need to remind yourself of all the adverse things that can happen to you. Don't be stagnant, even when you are in your home or a familiar place. Always keep pushing the envelope to put yourself out of the comfort zone.

Don't waste your energy

It is quite obvious to get drained after staying focused for a while, but you can't let fatigue set it. Make an effort to keep yourself hydrated and nourished. Give your brain enough oxygen to think and make accurate decisions. Sleep is also quite important, as insomnia might take your edge off. Though, scarcity of water or food in your body can also have a drastic impact on your decision-making as well.

Avoid an unwanted scenario like this by taking a proper care of your body. Eat, drink, sleep, and notice the sign of fatigue before it would take the hold of your body. Blurry vision, short breaths, bad temper, etc. are some common signs of fatigue.

Peripheral vision

This is the best-kept secret of situational awareness that even the experts don't share. It has been proven by psychologists that you might draw unwanted attention to a possible threat while looking directly at them. After getting engaged by your initial eye-contact, the possible threat might attack you.

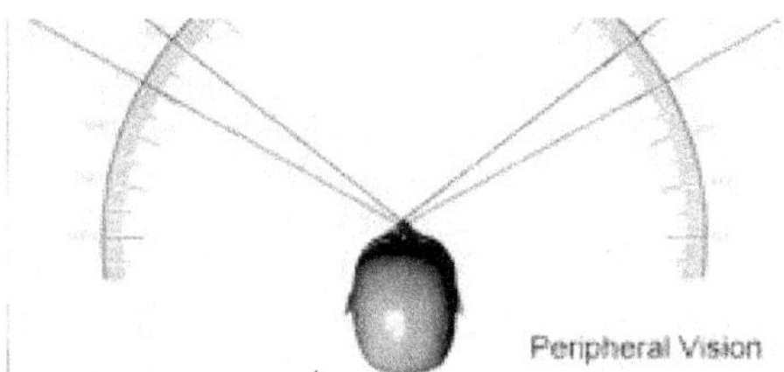

To avoid such an unwanted attention, try to develop your peripheral vision. That is, learn the art of seeing something from the sides. This might look strange in the beginning, but after a while, you can simply master this art.

If you would keep looking at a few people (or even animals) directly, then they might approach you. With the help of peripheral vision, you can attain a tactical advantage and can attack someone else unexpectedly.

All of this will certainly help you a lot to stay focused and attentive during an adverse situation. Although, you can't simply change yourself just like that! Remember, Rome was not built in a day. After days of practice, you would be able to master this art. After getting aware of your surroundings, learn how you can predict an upcoming event in the next chapter.

Chapter 5 – Be Aware In An Adverse Environment

Too many times, attaining knowledge regarding your environment is not enough. Though after staying focused you can get to know more about an upcoming threat, but it can also take you off-guard. The best way to deal with a dangerous situation is by getting yourself familiar with it.

Only after getting to know about the threat and its associated environment, you can come up with a plan of action. Consider these steps in mind while trying to take this crucial step.

Maintain your personal space

Your personal space can be of a great help while working on your situational awareness. We all have our own space that we like to maintain. Whenever we are surrounded by people, they invade our personal space. In order to harness your SA skills, you need to identify your own space and get to know immediately whenever any foreign entity enters your space.

It doesn't matter if you are in a mall or a park, but you should never let go of your personal guard. It is usually of an arm's length, but might change from one situation to another. If a person crosses that distance, then you need to identify their intention and come up with a plan as fast as you can.

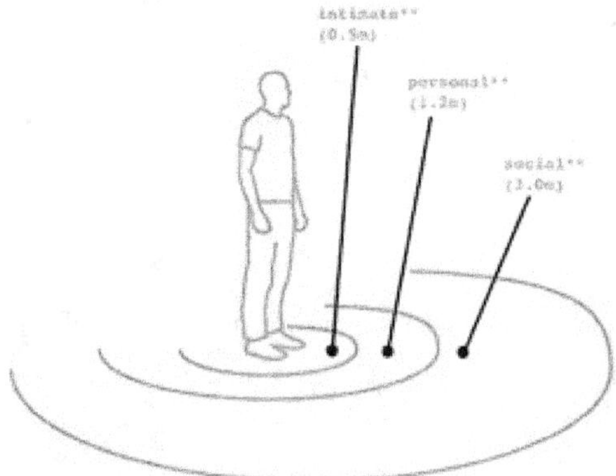

If someone crosses your space, try to look for a weapon or any other sign of a threat. Focus on their hands and examine if they are carrying a weapon or making a fist to attack you. Try to read their facial expression, as you can learn their true intentions from it easily.

Predicting the upcoming events

After analyzing so much, you would be able to easily predict the upcoming events around you. This is one of the key benefits of situational awareness. You can be a few steps ahead of others and learn from every small thing around you.

Start by creating a baseline of the situation, which will let you know how a normal behavior would seem like. Subsequently, consider that baseline in mind while comparing it with the ongoing changes and predict the upcoming events. This will make you prepared for the unknown and nothing would take you by surprise.

Start from the basics (the obvious) things and gradually harness your sixth sense. For instance, if you see two individuals arguing with each other, you might predict of this turning into a fight, giving you a chance to take subsequent actions. If you see a car stopping by, then you might predict someone opening the gates, and so on.

This would be of a great help to you in the wild as well. For instance, if you see a lake around, then chances are that you might stumble upon some wild animals as well. If the water is still, chances are that there could be a predator underneath, etc.

Go with your gut feeling

This is something we all are told of ever since we were kids. Sometimes, we all get a gut feeling about something. Due to possible threats or the knowledge of the obvious, we try to shake it. When it comes to survival, never try to shake off your gut feelings.

There are times when you just know what to do. You might not be aware of the surrounding environment or the stimuli, but you sense danger and react a certain way. Humans have a "sixth sense" and they can sense danger just like most of the other animals.

Trust your gut at the time of any dangerous situation and make that daring move. It might appear a little irrational at times, but don't shake it. It might end up saving your life one day.

Position yourself correctly

The way you walk or where you simply stand or sit can sometimes play a vital role in situational awareness. For instance, if you are in a crowded place and would like to see what everyone is doing, then you should move towards the center and have your back to a wall. This will let you have a clear view and you can easily analyze the situation.

The moment you enter a new environment, try to analyze it quickly and think of an optimum position to get the maximum view. Though at the same time, if the situation demands, you should make sure that you are not getting noticed by others while watching them.

Also, positioning yourself near exits would give you an added advantage. It would be convenient for you to see the incoming moment while making it easier for you to escape as well.

Your position, gut feeling, combined with your newly attained knowledge of predicting future events can certainly help you change the game. This is what makes situational awareness so vital.

After applying these key elements, you can certainly learn to act wisely and come out as a survivor. Get to know about some quick tricks to harness your SA skills in the next section.

Chapter 6 – Tips To Improve Your Situational Awareness

We are sure that by now you must be well-aware of situational awareness and how you can improve your SA skills. To help you, we have come up with some easy tips and tricks that can help you harness your situational awareness.

- Whenever you are in the middle of an emergency situation, keep monitoring the performance of everyone around you. If you are surrounded by your loved ones, then you should make an effort to make it easier for them as well. Keep checking their vitals while considering the surrounding environment in mind to save them.

- Don't cycle or run continuously for hours in the middle of a disaster. Keep an eye on your fatigue level and keep nourishing yourself on regular intervals.

- Avoid overload as much as you can. Situational overload can cause high stress and might increase the occurrence of errors. Don't overburden yourself with too many things. Not only will it distract you, but it would also consume your energy without producing any results.

- Learn to observe things silently. Those who are good listeners rarely get noticed by the crowd. You can easily go unnoticed and gain extensive information about your surroundings while observing people and other entities.

- Confusion would be your worst enemy. While it is good to think of various alternatives and their outcomes, you need to make a decision as fast as you can. A confused mind will never let you harness your situational awareness.

- Whenever you are interacting with others, focus on their body language. Always try to get into their heads and try to analyze a situation from their perspective.

- Develop your common senses. See, hear, and smell differently and learn to focus on every sense without getting confused.

- While analyzing a situation, you might be surrounded by plenty of unwanted things. Learn to filter out the things that are no longer relevant to you, so that you can focus on what matters the most.

- Learn how to relax your mind. Stress and exertion can hinder your decision-making abilities and you might end up making a mistake. Try to think of a peaceful place or even chant a mantra if it helps you to relax your senses.

- In order to attain a peaceful mind, you should try to meditate. This would help you drastically during an emergency situation. Meditation can help you to relax your mind and let you learn how you can focus on certain aspects while filtering everything around it. If you can master this art, then it can definitely boost your SA skills.

- Don't rely on technology too much. Most of the new-age tools that we all are surrounded with inhibit our natural situational awareness. These days, instead of going with their gut while exploring a city, people usually go with their GPS. Move out of your smartphone-zone if you want to work on your situational awareness.

- Work on your memory and body language. When you are observing someone else, chances are that you might be getting observed by them as well. Always try to have a neutral stand and keep making notes about certain things in your brain.

- Take good care of your body and mind. Try to run every morning in order to keep your body in its best shape. Running can drastically help you to build your immune system. It has plenty of other benefits as well. It can help you stay focused and harness your natural instinct. As humans, we all are born to run. Don't let it fade away.

We are sure that after working on these hacks, you can definitely level-up your situational awareness game. It is an art that can only be mastered with time. Follow this comprehensive guide and take one step at a time to a safer and healthier tomorrow!

Conclusion

Congratulations for completing this guide so fast! We are sure you must have had a great time working on your Situational Awareness skills. It is definitely a vital practice that can help you a lot to save your life.

We live in an unpredictable world and chances are that you might face an unexpected situation out of the blue. In order to survive or simply avoid a dangerous situation, you would definitely need the assistance of your situational awareness skills.

To help you, we have come up with this extensive guide. We have provided a step-wise walkthrough of how one can develop their situational awareness and face an urban or rural disaster. Additionally, to help you fight a battle, we made you familiar with the combat rule of three.

Follow every step sequentially and take the assistance of our easy tips and tricks in order to make it work. From accessing an unknown environment to coming up with a foolproof plan, you can certainly do it all. Take it one step at a time and develop your situational awareness with us. You never know, it might end up saving your life one day!

FREE Bonus Reminder

If you have not grabbed it yet, please go ahead and download your special bonus report
"Preppers Survival Guide. Proven Tactics For Armed Incounters!"

Simply Click the Button Below

OR **Go to This Page**

http://preppersliving.com/free

BONUS #2: More Free & Discounted Books & Products

Do you want to receive more Free/Discounted Books or Products?

We have a mailing list where we send out our new Books or Products
when they go free or with a discount on Amazon. Click on the link below
to sign up for Free & Discount Book & Product Promotions.

=> Sign Up for Free & Discount Book & Product Promotions <=

OR Go to this URL

http://zbit.ly/1WBb1Ek

www.ingramcontent.com/pod-product-compliance
Lightning Source LLC
Chambersburg PA
CBHW061327250726
48657CB00003B/1081